FAST FORWARD

MALCOLM BURTON

Fast Forward

Copyright © 2016 by Malcolm Burton

All rights reserved. No part of this book may be reproduced or transmitted in any form or by any means without written permission of the author.

ISBN-13: 978-0-9968715-5-6

Printed in the United States of America

RevMedia Publishing

PO BOX 5172, Kingwood, TX 77325

No part of this book may be reproduced or transmitted in any form or by any means, electronic or mechanical—including photocopying, recording, or by any information storage and retrieval system—without permission in writing from the publisher.

Unless otherwise noted, all Scripture references are taken from the New King James Version, Thomas Nelson Publishing Company, Nashville, TN © 1980. Used by permission.

Why I Wrote This Book

Foundation Text: *"Work out your own salvation with fear and trembling; for it is God who works in you both to will and to do for His good pleasure,"* (Philippians 2:13-14).

I have spiritual children.

Some were birthed under my ministry.

Others have chosen me as a spiritual father.

One of these spiritual children called me Sunday morning, January 4, 2015. The Holy Spirit had spoken and she called me to share His statement, "Fast Forward."

Maybe you are in the same season as I am. You may have been "bogged down" by the events of life.

You may be stuck in a spot of "rewinding" painful events. The Holy Spirit is saying, *"Fast Forward!"*

The Christian life is composed of two elements: God's part and our part.

I am not telling you moving forward is easy. I am finding it difficult, but I believe there are steps to moving into *"Fast Forward."*

Thank you for joining me on the journey to better days.

It is time to *Fast Forward.*

Malcolm Burton
Madison County, Texas

Table of Contents

Deliberately Choose God's Way 7
Run With Winning As Your Goal 9
Drop Those Extra Pounds 11
Shift Your Focus To Success 13
Establish Clear Objectives 15
Live Today While Looking Into Tomorrow 17
Move Forward…No Matter What 19
Don't Bring Yesterday Into Today 21
Recommit Yourself To The Word of God 23
Reject Fear of What Lies Ahead 25
Know Your Enemy and Expect to Defeat Him 27
See Struggle as Seasonal, Not Eternal 29
Understand God Is Your Place of Safety 31
Study Past Victories 33
Trust The Word of God 35
Receive Peace 37
Walk In Prosperity 39
Choose Your Focus 41
Celebrate Your Righteous Confidence 43
Believe and Obey Prophetic Decrees 45
Forgive Others and Forgive The Process 47
Behave Like A Winner 49
Forgive To Release Financial Favor 53
Constantly Feed Your Faith 57
Recognize You Are In A Faith Fight 61
Refuse Confusion 63
Do Not Make Life Harder Than It Has To Be 67
Honor The Law of The Seed 69
Consider Your Location 73
Learn The Power of Ongoing Forgiveness 77
Respect The Law of Honor 81

1

Deliberately Choose God's Way

"O' God, you are my God. At dawn I search for you. My soul thirsts for you. My body longs for you in a dry thirsty land where there is no water," (Psalm 63:1, God's Word Translation).

Human Nature Screams For Supremacy.

Our humanity always wants its way. It will not govern itself; it must be governed. Our only pathway into success is moving in His direction.

Doing things God's way will not happen automatically. You will have to deliberately make the decision to go God's way. As you master the discipline of doing things God's way you will find it becoming easier because of the law of momentum.

Wisdom Declaration: "You are my God. You have my best interest in mind. I will do things your way. Living in agreement with you will produce rewards beyond my imagination. I speak this by faith in The Name of Jesus."

2

Run With Winning As Your Goal

"Do you not know that in a race all the runners compete, but (only) one receives the prize? So run (your race) that you may lay hold (of the prize) and make it yours," (1 Corinthians 9:24, The Amplified Bible).

America Loves A Winner.

Yet I find American society in a strange place. A generation of people has been raised up who want to be declared winners regardless of their outcome. As a result of this societal thinking I was not terribly surprised to see children receiving trophies just for showing up.

My generation was different. Trophies were only given to winning teams. My youngest son's high school gave "letter jackets" to every member of the team. My generation required participation in 75% of football and basketball quarters. Baseball required an appearance in 75% of games.

Track required a "letterman" to score a point in the district track meet. In our athletic district points were given for places 1-6 in the track and field events. There were eight teams in our district. I remember being elated when the first two shot-put contestants "scratched." I knew then I only had to not "foul" on the toss in order to be a letterman. I did the minimum and was rewarded with a jacket bearing a likeness of a shot put. The jacket was actually ugly, but it was mine and I proudly wore it.

Harness the power of focus today. Run the race with patient endurance. Our Lord has promised great reward to the faithful.

Pray to win today.

Pray to win everyday.

Wisdom Declaration: "The Word of God promises great reward to those who choose to run the race with dogged determination. I am running the race of life with the goal of scriptural success in mind. My faith is active and focused. By faith in the power of the Name of Jesus I declare I will achieve my goals."

3

Drop Those Extra Pounds

"Therefore then, since we are surrounded by so great a cloud of witnesses (who have borne testimony to the Truth) let us strip off and throw aside every encumbrance (unnecessary weight) and that sin that so readily (deftly and cleverly) clings to and entangles us, and let us run with patient endurance and steady and active persistence the appointed course of the race that is set before us," (Hebrews 12:1, Amplified Bible).

I Have Carried Unnecessary Weight.

Yes, I am speaking of physical weight. But there are even more debilitating weights to carry. Spiritual and emotional weights have held me down.

Christmas can be a time of weight gain for many people. Somehow I lost 11 pounds from December 15-29. But I refused to live under delusion…*I must pay attention to my weight.*

Television viewers in the United States are constantly barraged with messages of the positive benefits of weight loss. Each advertisement offers a different solution to the same problem.

Believers are redeemed people. Jesus bought us back from the system of sin. We are not so often bothered by sin as we are by weights…*things God didn't design us to carry.*

The Christian community even has the benefit of living in freedom from the weight of bad decisions and false guilt.

Ask yourself, "What extra pounds am I carrying?" Are you carrying about pounds of known sin? If so, simple repentance can free you. Is a generational curse, something that has always plagued your family, working against your life? Speak forth your own deliverance.

Maybe you are feeling the fatigue brought about by carrying around pounds of disappointment and rejection. This is not the plan of God for your life.

Drop those extra pounds today!

Wisdom Declaration: "Jesus solved the sin question for me. I believe He also has provided the pathway to living in victory. I choose to set aside the weights of disappointment and failure. Whom The Son has set free is free. I receive my freedom through the work of Jesus. It is done!"

4

Shift Your Focus To Success

"This Book of the Law shall not depart from your mouth, but you shall meditate in it day and night, that you may observe to do according to all that is written in it. For then you will make your way prosperous, and then you will have good success," (Joshua 1:8).

Success Is Not An Automatic.

Success is both a destination and a choice. Success must be discerned and chosen. The Kingdom of God is designed to produce success in the life of the believer.

Let me assert a bold opinion: Success is guaranteed for those who live a Kingdom lifestyle.

The Kingdom of God was established in such a way as to reward bold faith. Never, not one time, have I been disappointed with the results I received when I moved in bold faith. Bold faith can only be manifest by those who highly honor The Word of God. This will work for you, too.

Shift your thinking from viewing The Bible as only a moral compass to understanding it as the success manual it is. When you do this the words of Joshua will become realized in your life.

The plan of God for you is a good one. When you discover His plan of blessing for your life you will literally sense your faith rising.

Choose to walk the highway of Kingdom prosperity today. It will lead you to the types of success your heart craves.

Wisdom Declaration: "When God created man it was clear that He desired relationship with His creation. Holy Spirit, I am in fellowship with you today. Thank You for revealing the plan of God for my life. Thank you for creating the Jesus life within me. I trust You because I know you keep Your promises. I receive by faith in The Name of Jesus. Amen."

5

Establish Clear Objectives

"One thing I have desired of the Lord, that will I seek: That I may dwell in the house of The Lord all the days of my life, to behold the beauty of The Lord, and to inquire in His temple," (Psalm 27:4).

Change Occurs In The Presence of God.

My children are somewhat like me because they spend time with me. My thinking shaped much of their world view.

When I spend time with God I begin to think like Him. I even begin to behave like Him.

King David was a man of many interests. But his ultimate goal was spending time in God's presence. The Sweet Psalmist of Israel makes the power of choice clear to all who read his writings.

Father God is a person who understands and practices goal-setting. He sent Jesus to earth with a goal of redeeming mankind and restoring humanity to a place of fellowship with Him.

When Jesus declared "it is finished" He was saying, "I have achieved my goal. The debt of sin is paid. Mankind now has a right to relationship with The Father."

My greatest goal is living a life that causes Jesus to say, "Well done." The highest form of success is a life that honors The Lord.

Take some time to prayerfully consider your life goals.

Wisdom Declaration: "As I spend more time with my Father God I become more like Him. I choose to think the thoughts of God today. I will make the moment-by-moment decision to consider His opinion in all I think, say and do. My life will improve at the speed of my spoken words of faith. The wisdom of The Word of God is lighting my pathway. The Holy Spirit is constantly revealing Jesus to me. I say what I believe in The Name of Jesus. So be it!"

6

Live Today While Looking Into Tomorrow

"Forgetting those things which are behind and reaching forward to those things which are ahead," (Philippians 3:13).

"Forget About It!"

We hear this forceful maxim repeated on a daily basis. There is a grain of truth in this advice concerning dealing with the past. But it is not the whole truth.

The Christian Life is a balancing act. Completely forget the past and you will find yourself subject to repeating mistakes. By deliberately dwelling on past heartaches you will never fully know the joy of God that is yours as a believer.

Dr. Mike Murdock once told me, "Yesterday is in the tomb. Tomorrow is in the womb. Look forward." That has proven to be remarkably powerful advice

Jesus taught us that offense will come. However, He also taught us to live above offense by choosing to forgive and move on.

Stir your expectation for better things.

Wisdom Declaration: "I can do nothing about my past. But I can establish my future. I declare my future will be better than my past. The knowledge of God is growing in me. I have learned from past mistakes and will not repeat them. I will not concentrate upon the past but focus upon my desired outcome. The Lord blesses my life and removes all sorrow. I am thankful. Amen."

7

Move Forward…No Matter What

"Press toward the goal for the prize of the upward call of God in Christ Jesus," (Philippians 3:14).

Direction Is A Decision.

We all have painful things in our past. As you read these words, you may hurt in this moment.

I am by no means minimizing your pain. I am, however, exhorting you to obey The Holy Spirit.

Too many people are living on "pause." Their life is a poorly focused thing based upon a frozen frame from the picture of life they constantly hold before them.

A married couple came to me for counsel. They had been together over 30 years. Their life was one of prosperity and social position. Even so, they lived with incredible pain between the two of them based upon disappointment that was never forgiven.

These marvelous people were frozen in time. On the day their first child was born, doctors said her labor had ceased and the child was not arriving any time soon. The husband left his sleeping wife at the hospital and went home to shower and change clothes. Instead of being right back as planned, he fell fast asleep and did not receive the phone call advising him he was needed at the hospital. The child was born while he was home sleeping

She routinely declared he could not be depended on. He would then call her "an unforgiving shrew." Each day revolved around mutual offense that was never forgiven.

These beautiful people were living "on pause." If this describes you it is time to "Fast Forward" and get on with God.

Wisdom Declaration: "I choose to live my life in the moment. I will not be bound by my past. Faith is my portion. Unbelief is not part of my life. I choose to not be victimized. I am a victor. Prizes are ahead for me as I pursue the plan of God for my life. The blessings of God are my portion and I refuse to live beneath my Kingdom privilege. I am fast-forwarding to my new day. I am blessed and I will be a blessing. I speak this in the Name of Jesus."

8

Don't Bring Yesterday Into Today

"For David, after he had served is own generation by the will of God, fell asleep, was buried with his fathers, and saw corruption (decay). (Acts 13:36).

The Spirit Realm Is Unlimited.

My children love to tease me. One of our family jokes is, "Star Trek has been very good to Dad. He learned physics by watching." It was there I learned that every human is restricted by the time space compendium. Jean Luc Picard taught me the truth.

We can only do things in the moment. David's ministry served His generation during his time on earth. Life is "now."

Yet, we seem to repeatedly fail into the trap of not letting go of the past. I am speaking from personal experience on this one.

I know what it is like to live "on pause." I went through a time when shame and embarrassment caused me to put my life on hold. I could not seem to get past the moment of failure. Emotionally I felt as if the failure I experienced had just happened. As King David said, my sin was *"...forever before me,"* (Psalm 51:3).

Now I know what it is like to live in freedom. My first step out of bondage was to hit the fast-forward button. I had to choose to move into the moment. I had to decide to change my thinking. I am no longer focused on the past. I am obsessed with where God is taking me.

Shift your focus. Stop binding God with your words. Shake off your past. Take the limits off God. Choose to move into your new season.

Wisdom Declaration: "I am not a sinner. I am a saint who occasionally sins. I do not have to sin. If I sin I have an advocate with God The Father, Jesus Christ The Righteous. His blood has been applied to The Mercy Seat. His blood continually declares I am forgiven and calls me to righteous living. The price has been paid. I am redeemed from my past. I choose to walk into my future with The Holy Spirit. My life is a good one and getting better each day. I speak this by faith in The Name of Jesus our Lord and Savior."

9

Recommit Yourself To The Word of God

"Study to show yourself approved unto God, a workman who does not need to be ashamed, rightly dividing the word of truth," (2 Timothy 2:15).

The Bible Is A Supernatural Book.

The Word of God Is Unique. It produces fruit nothing else can produce. The Word holds a spot in the believer that nothing else can occupy. There is no substitute for The Word of God. Prayer cannot replace time spent pondering the Word of God. Worship cannot replace the necessity of ingesting The Word of God.

Nothing has changed my life like the entrance of the Word of God. I was saved at an early age. I was baptized in The Holy Spirit at the age of 10, but I grew up among a group of people who valued an emotional experience with God more than the eternally life-changing work of The Word of God.

Nothing will change your life like the entrance of the Word of God. The Word of God brings the wisdom necessary for success in life. The Word of God releases light to the dark places we encounter. The Word of God gives the outline we need for experiencing supernatural success in life.

One of my daily goals is spending time reading and studying the Word of God. I approach The Word of God in the power of The Holy Spirit as a supernatural learner. I expect God to give me insight that produces an incredible lifestyle.

Make time for The Word of God each day. You will never regret the time you invest in the Word of God.

Wisdom Declaration: "The Word of God is working mightily in me. It is making me wiser than the enemies that oppose me. It is lighting my pathway. It is creating understanding within me. It is continually giving me the direction I need to succeed in every area of life. Jesus built His Church upon revelation knowledge of The Word of God. I declare that I am a person of revelation knowledge. His Word is my wisdom. The Word of God is achieving an even higher place in my life today. I have hidden His Word in my heart. Because of this truth I will not sin against Him today. I declare these things through my faith in The Word of The Resurrected Christ, Jesus my Lord, God and King."

10

Reject Fear of What Lies Ahead

"Do not fear, for I am with you; Do not anxiously look about you, for I am your God. I will strengthen you, surely I will help you. Surely I will uphold you with My righteous right hand," (Isaiah 41:10).

Faith Displaces Fear.

There are two types of fear: Reasonable and unreasonable. It is reasonable that you fear falling off a roof, wrecking your car, or picking up a hot object. It is unreasonable fear that causes people to look to the future with a sense that they have no real hope.

My Mom was a member of my congregation for the final 20-plus years of her life on earth. She constantly remarked how blessed she was to sit under the ministry of a teaching pastor.

I noticed remarkable growth in both Mom and Dad during the years they were with me. Mom was a product of parents who lived through The Great Depression. She grew up in an environment that fostered the thought that "hard times" were "just around the corner."

This uncertainty concerning financial matters caused her constant stress until she learned the power of the abiding presence of The Holy Spirit. Peace began to manifest in her life when she came to understanding that circumstances had no direct bearing on her relationship with God.

Victory came when Mom learned that her financial Seed was speaking for her and creating advantages of which she might not be aware. After a Sunday service, Mom came to me in tears. "Why didn't they tell me?" she asked.

"Tell you what?" I asked in return.

"Why didn't they tell me a tither should expect the blessings of God to work in her life?"

In an attempt to be fair to her previous pastors while ministering comfort to her I honestly said, "Either they didn't know, or they were afraid to attach a blessing to the command to bring the whole tithe into the storehouse. Mom, maybe they felt pressured that fulfilling the promise of God somehow fell upon them."

Mom's unspoken fear was then revealed. "Daddy and I are getting old. Is it possible God could give us a debt-free home?"

"Yes, it is. Your Seed is speaking for you and creating a supernatural situation for you."

At the time she went to heaven, Mom and Dad owned two homes. Her Seed really was speaking for her.

The plan of God for you is a good one. Expect His best today.

Wisdom Declaration: "The God of my faith is eternally existent. While I do not fully comprehend it, I believe He exists in both my now and my future. I believe Jesus has gone ahead of me. He has created opportunities for me on earth and an eternal home in heaven. My trust is in The Lord, The Maker of Heaven and Earth. I will not fear what man can do to me. Amen."

11

Know Your Enemy and Expect to Defeat Him

"For we wrestle not against flesh and blood but against principalities, against powers, against the rulers of darkness of this world, against spiritual wickedness in high places. Wherefore take unto you the whole armor of God that you may be able to withstand in the evil day, and having done all to stand, stand..." (Ephesians 6:12-14).

The Price Of Freedom Is Vigilance.

The United States has The CIA. Israel has Mossad. England has MI-6 (James Bond).

The responsibility of these agencies is to study and anticipate the activities of the enemies of their respective nations. These intelligence offices report to the civilian leadership of the government what they believe to be the plans and intentions of enemy states.

I have to constantly remind myself that I am not fighting people. Even if am struggling against people who are motivated by destructive reasoning, my battle is still with demon spirits...*not with the people being used by satan to bring hurt or harm to my life.*

Our battle is against a demonic hierarchy, not people. We must pray against the structure, not the people representing it.

Take a moment to ask The Holy Spirit, "Will you please reveal the strategies being used against me?" He speaks to those who speak to Him. James, the brother of Jesus, tells us God does not withhold wisdom from those who earnestly seek His knowledge (Read James 1:5).

When your enemy is revealed, refuse to be intimidated. Declare your expectation of victory over him.

> **Wisdom Declaration:** "I have faith. The Bible says faith produces victory over all evil things. It is not the will of God that I live with sickness, financial lack or emotional torment. This is the day I choose to move to a better place in God. Amen!"

12

Struggle Is Seasonal, Not Eternal

"His favor is for life; Weeping may endure for a night, but joy comes in the morning," (Psalm 30:5B).

You Are Designed For Victory.

Life contains struggle. I have struggled, but I do not struggle every day. When I am in a time of struggle, I expect it to come to an end. I speak that expectation aloud.

Your faith declaration does not have to be elaborate. It can be something so simple as, "I expect this season of struggle to swiftly come to an end."

Your suffering is not the will of God for your life. Believers are living under grace. The wrath of God is reserved for the sinner, not the believer.

I do not routinely expect to have hard days. The Bible says, *"Good understanding gives favor; but the way of the transgressor is hard,"* (Proverbs 13:15, King James 2000 Bible).

The good news is that, even if we do anger God, it is a momentary thing. His favor is for a lifetime. Another interpretation of this verse could be, "Life in Him is a place of favor."

Wisdom Declaration: "Today I will work on my confession. Throughout this day I will declare, "I have favor with God and man. Favor is going before me creating opportunities that will bring me success in every area of my life and ministry."

13

Understand God Is Your Place of Safety

"You are my hiding place; You shall preserve me from trouble; You shall surround me with songs of deliverance," (Psalm 32:7).

I Love The Church.

I have served as a pastor for over 40 years. I love the people God places under my care. It is not an exaggeration for me to say, that I have an interest in the church around the world.

Travel to Communist countries brings with it an element of peril. I expressed concern before my first trip to China. Pastor Sulynn Hewlett said, "The safest place on earth is in the will of God. If we are in the will of God we will be safe wherever we go. If we are out of the will of God we are unsafe in our own living room."

We have a hiding place in God. He promises to preserve us from trouble. Condition the atmosphere by joining The Holy Spirit in singing songs that celebrate your deliverance.

As much as I love the universal church, it is not a place without flaws. My home church was one such place. As a result of her upbringing, my Mom believed salvation was hard to attain and easy to lose. Truthfully, it is just the opposite.

Due to this harsh theology, Mom did not really discover the goodness of God until she was in her late 50's. She told me she often suffered from unreasonable fear. Chief among them was being left alone.

Jesus will never leave you alone. Emotional torment is defeated in the presence of God. Run into the Secret Place of fellowship with Him today.

Wisdom Declaration: "Father God, you are my hiding place. You are my place of safety. In your presence I find deliverance from fear. I am growing in my knowledge of You. Thank you from keeping me safe from all harm."

14

Study Past Victories

"Your servant slew both the lion and the bear; and this uncircumcised Philistine shall be to me as one of them, seeing he has defied the armies of The Living God," (1 Samuel 17:6).

Pain Has A Voice.

Pain always screams for attention. Current pain wants to be discussed. Doing so is completely counterproductive.

Do not look back to study and recall pain. Look back for the purpose of studying victories. Your faith-level will increase as you recall what God has done.

If you are fighting illness, look back to the times when He healed your body. If you are fighting heartache, look back to the times when God brought you to places of great joy. If you are under financial pressure, look back to the days when God brought you through the hard place.

Your expectation will rise and victory will come into sight.

Wisdom Declaration: "Jesus is my healer. He has proven Himself to be my healer in previous times and is doing so right now. He has already given me victory over sin, sickness and pre-mature death. I claim His victory as my own in Him. Physical pain is not for me. Emotional torment is not His plan for me. I am healed. I am whole."

15

Trust The Word of God

The Word Can Be Trusted.

I grew up in the church. I grew up around people who loved God. They especially loved emotional preaching. I do not mean to be critical, but there was not much knowledge of The Word of God.

My lifelong quest continues to be knowing God through His Word. This ambition began at an early age. During the summer I turned 10, I read Psalm 63:6, "When I remember thee upon my bed, I meditate on thee during the night watches." In that moment the Word of God came alive to me. It described exactly what I was doing. I was profoundly impacted by understanding I was doing something that pleased God.

The Word of God Contains The Power of God.

The Word of God produces personal stability. *"Blessed is the man who trusts in the Lord, and whose hope is in the Lord. For he shall be like a tree planted by the waters which spreads out its roots by the river, and will not fear when heat comes; But its leaf will be green; and will not be anxious in the year of drought, nor will cease from yielding fruit,"* (Jeremiah 17:7-8).

The Word of God gives us the ability to think the thoughts of God. *"For we ourselves were also once foolish, disobedient, deceived, serving various lusts and pleasures, living in malice and envy, hateful and hating one another. But when the kindness and the love of God our Savior toward man appeared, not by works of righteousness which we have done, but according to His mercy He saved us, through the washing of regeneration and renewing of the Holy Spirit, whom He poured out on us abundantly through Jesus Christ our Savior, that having been justified by His grace we should become heirs according to the hope of eternal life,"* (Titus 3:3-7).

Foolish thinking need not be part of our lifestyle. We have been given the authority and ability to think on a higher plane.

Wisdom Declaration: The Word of God produces assurance that I will never be separated from the love of God. I will not be bogged down in the morass of my human opinions. I am on course and up to speed with God.

16

Receive Peace

Peace Is Not The Absence Of Conflict.

Peace Is The Presence Of God During Conflict.

God says His plan is to shake things up. Yes, satanic attack is part of the Christian life. It is not the will of God that His people suffer loss, but when they do, His promise is restoration and peace of mind.

When will this happen? After the outpouring of The Holy Spirit. *"Until the Spirit is poured upon us from on high, And the wilderness becomes a fruitful field, And the fruitful field is counted as a forest,"* (Isaiah 32:6).

The fruitless becomes fruitful

The mourning will become joyful.

The unproductive becomes productive.

It Is The Will of God That We Live In Peace. Allow this series of promises to enter your spirit.

1. **Justice Will Reign In The Place of Lawlessness.**
   "Then justice will dwell in the wilderness,

2. **Right Conduct Will Manifest In The Workplace.**

And righteousness remain in the fruitful field.

3. **Righteousness Will Produce Peace, Quiet and Assurance of Blessing.** [17]The work of righteousness will be peace, And the effect of righteousness, quietness and assurance forever.

4. **Peace and Safety Will Reign Over The Faithful During Times of Calamity.** [18]My people will dwell in a peaceful habitation, In secure dwellings, and in quiet resting places, [19]Though hail comes down on the forest, And the city is brought low in humiliation.

5. **Peaceful Prosperity Will Be The Portion of Those Who Do Business With God.** [20]Blessed are you who sow beside all waters, Who send out freely the feet of the ox and the donkey," (Isaiah 32:16-20).

Wisdom Declaration: "Jesus paid the price to purchase my mental and emotional peace when He endured the tormenting pain of the crown of thorns. I will walk in the fullness of His peace today."

17

Walk In Prosperity

It Is The Will of God That We Live In Prosperity.

"Beloved, I pray that you may prosper in all things and be in health, just as your soul prospers. 3 For I rejoiced greatly when brethren came and testified of the truth that is in you, just as you walk in the truth. I have no greater joy than to hear that my children walk in truth," (3 John 2).

John celebrated the prosperity of his spiritual children. He had received reports they were prospering in every area of their lives. Apostle John celebrated that they were "getting it right."

John teaches us prosperity comes from the truth living within us. It is the truth that God wants us to prosper in "The Big Three."

God wants us living in material prosperity so we can care for our families, leave a legacy for our grandchildren and fully fund the work of The Kingdom.

God wants us to prosper in our health. I love the message of healing, but health is actually God's preference for His people. Healing came as the answer to when we fall out of health.

There is no challenge within Christianity that God wants His people to prosper in their relationship with Him. All of Christianity teaches God wants to know and be involved with His children.

The debate comes as to how involved God desires to be. All seem to believe he will save. Fewer believe health is His will, and even fewer still believe prosperity is His will for every believer.

Yet, His Word is clear. God wants His people to prosper on the outside (physically and financially) as He desires us to prosper on the inside (our soul area).

The choice is ours.

Wisdom Declaration: "I believe it is the will of God that I prosper in every area of my life. Today I declare that I am financially prosperous. The blessings of Abraham are mine. I will lend and not borrow. I am a liberal giver, and the liberal giver is a person of financial increase. I am physically prosperous. My physical strength operates at a high level. I have plenty of energy. I have all these things because my soul is prospering in the knowledge of God and His Word."

18

Choose Your Focus

Set Your Mind on Things Above.

We have a unique possibility as believers.

We have the ability to be alive unto our God.

We do not simply have the ability to be dead to sin. We have been given the ability to be overcomers in every area of life, but the door into success in The Kingdom swings on focus.

Contrary to what some think and advocate, there are few automatics in The Kingdom. Focus is required. Consider this proof text. *"If then you were raised with Christ, seek those things which are above, where Christ is, sitting at the right hand of God,"* (Colossians 3:1).

The focus of the believer must be on the spirit realm in order to have success in the earth realm. *"Set your mind on things above, not on things on the earth."* Colossians 3:2).

Revelation comes in so many ways. One amazing revelation came through observing the life of Pastor Ben Priest. Ben had been "one bad dude." He was a leader in the Bandidos Outlaw Motorcycle Gang. His salvation experience did not sit well with his former cohorts in crime.

One outlaw threatened to kill Ben if he did not renounce Jesus.

Ben refused.

Ben made a remarkable statement, "You can't kill a dead man." The Apostle Paul had already convinced Ben, *"For you died, and your life is hidden with Christ in God,"* (Colossians 3:3).

Focus Produces Right Choices.

We are as free as we choose to be.

We are as dead to sin as we choose to be.

We are as alive unto God as we choose to be.

Yes, Jesus will come again and we will appear with Him in glory. However, He already lives within us. He desires we use our focus so He may be glorified in all we say and do.

"When Christ who is our life appears, then you also will appear with Him in glory," (Colossians 3:1-4).

Men and women fail because of *broken* focus.

Men and women succeed because of *chosen* focus.

Wisdom Declaration: "Even as I go about my daily tasks, my thoughts are on things above. I am focused like a laser upon the things of God. My focus will not be broken by anyone or anything. The glory of God will be revealed through my life today."

19

Celebrate Your Righteous Confidence

God Loves You.

Never lose sight of this elementary truth.

Every good thing we receive flows from the love of God.

I didn't hear much of the love of God growing up. The God I met and came to know and love was much more gracious than the God my elders described.

Condemnation was a constant struggle within my heart because of negative teaching. The Christian life was never designed to be such a thing.

That is not the case today. I live a life free of guilt. I am not living a lifestyle of sin. Therefore, there is nothing satan can use to accuse me.

Believers do still sin, and when we do our heart would condemn us. Even so, there is a resolution for these failures. We must walk in revelation knowledge of the Word of God.

Unresolved Condemnation Damages Our Confidence In Our Relationship With God. Condemnation is not our portion. "There is therefore now no condemnation to those who are in Christ Jesus, who do not walk according to the flesh, but according to the Spirit," (Romans 8:1).

The love of God is greater than the accusations of my human heart. *"For if our heart condemns us, God is greater than our heart, and knows all things,"* (1 John 3:20).

The remedy is to quickly repent and position ourselves in such a way that the powers of hell have no way of holding us in a place of failure. Then our heart cannot bind us to the error. *"Beloved, if our heart does not condemn us, we have confidence toward God. ²²And whatever we ask we receive from Him, because we keep His commandments and do those things that are pleasing in His sight,"* (1 John 3:21-22).

Providence is a beautiful word we don't use much these days. Providence is the manifestation of God's foresight and care for His people.

God knew condemnation would be a tool of the devil. He has given us grace to overcome.

God knows what is best for us and stands ready to bring it to pass with our faith and agreement.

Wisdom Declaration: I will allow the Holy Spirit to guide my footsteps today. As I do I will find myself walking in the providential care of God. Nothing that happens today will surprise my God. His protection will keep me safe from traps, schemes and devices. This will be another day of great victory!

20

Believe and Obey Prophetic Decrees

I Believe In Prophetic Ministry.

Prophets of God are walking on the earth today.

Many individuals flow in the manifestation gift of prophecy.

Prophetic ministers do two things: They share insights and release anointings. *"So they arose early in the morning and went out into the Wilderness of Tekoa, and as they went out, Jehosophat stood and said, "Hear me O Judah and you inhabitants of Jerusalem. Believe in the Lord your God, and you shall be established; believe His prophets and you shall prosper,"* (2 Chronicles 20:20).

When we receive and attempt to incorporate these insights and anointing, our life becomes a prosperous place. Powerful things happen when we say "Amen" to the prophetic Word of The Lord.

Aman is Hebrew for believe.

Our "Amen" comes from aman.

We declare "Amen" to teaching and insights. When we do, it means more than just "I agree." It means, "I believe what you are saying." It goes deeper to, "Let this truth be established in my life."

What prophetic decrees have been offered over your life? Take a moment to think back. Consider the ones you felt to be most significant. Begin to think in terms of what you can do to help bring about these Divine directives.

For years I had a wrong idea. I had no understanding I had a role to play in bringing the prophetic word to pass in my life.

I fell for the bad doctrine of the day, "I will put this prophecy on the shelf. If it comes to pass, I will know it was really of God."

Not now. Today I ask, "Holy Spirit, what do I do to help bring this to pass?"

Wisdom Declaration: "Holy Spirit, I know you are a revealer. Heaven has spoken something it wants to happen on earth. Help me to remember the genuine prophetic words that have been spoken over my life. Reveal to me what I must do to play my part. As you give me insight I will move in quick obedience. I will do things your way!"

21

Forgive Others and Forgive The Process

To Be Forgiven We Must Forgive Others.

Forgiveness is not an easy thing, but it is necessary.

Forgiveness Is Conditional. Jesus made this very clear,

In order to be forgiven, we must forgive others. If we fail to forgive others we will stay in a place of suffering because we will not be free of the offense they inflicted upon us. *"For if you forgive men their trespasses, your heavenly Father will also forgive you. [15]But if you do not forgive men their trespasses, neither will your Father forgive your trespasses,"* (Matthew 6:14-15).

You may have suffered abuse. I can speak from personal experience that forgiving such heinous things is impossible without the help of God.

Some things are so awful you will have to forgive them each time you think of them. The good news is you will eventually stop thinking of them as your forgiveness of evil deeds releases healing into your life, *"Then Peter came to Him and said, "Lord, how often shall my brother sin against me, and I forgive him? Up to seven times?" [22]Jesus said to him, "I do not say to you, up to seven times, but up to seventy times seven."* (Matthew 18:21-22)

Bishop Corletta Vaughn leads a group of churches in the

Detroit, Michigan area. Her ministry efforts also take her to the nations of the earth where she meets with exceptional results.

She made a remarkable statement, "You may need to forgive God for the process." The thought jarred me.

We all know God has done nothing wrong. Why? Because we know He is incapable of wrongdoing.

But we also know many people incorrectly blame God for things, including the personal mess they have created. They instinctively know there is a price to pay for their wrongdoing, but they blame God for the suffering their own wrong decisions have caused.

God is only responsible for human suffering in the sense that He created the law of sowing and reaping. Roll your pain off onto His broad shoulders. Let Him be your burden bearer.

Wisdom Declaration: "Father, I know you are blameless. The pain I have suffered is not your will. You are a good father who does not want his children to experience pain. While other people may not be blameless, I choose to forgive them anyway. I will forgive freely, forcefully and forever. I am forgiven, and I choose to forgive others. I am free of past hurt and walk in joy today."

22

Behave Like A Winner

The Enemy of Your Faith Is Already Defeated.

We know Jesus died on the cross.

We know three days passed before His resurrection.

How many people know what really happened during that time?

We know from Scripture Jesus descended into the lower regions. Theologians argue if this is Paradise (aka Abraham's Bosom) or hell. One group contends he went to gehenna, the place of dead spirits. Others say he went to sheol, hell.

I do not believe he ministered a "second chance" to the unbelieving dead. I do believe he ministered "completion" to The Old Testament saints who died in faith. Whatever the case, we know He arose victorious over death, hell and the grave.

> *"But to each one of us grace was given according to the measure of Christ's gift. Therefore He says: "When He ascended on high, He led captivity captive, And gave gifts to men,"* (Ephesians 4:7-8)

The Bible tells us in Ephesians 4:8, "...*He led captivity captive*..." Simply put, Jesus came out of the grave and took captive everything that had the ability to take us captive.

This is why I can say, "We are as free as we choose to be." The price is paid. The pathway is made. All we need to do is accept the payment and choose to walk the path that leads to victory in life.

Note another important phrase in verse eight, "...*and gave gifts to men*..." These gifts are the Five-Fold Ministries of The Church.

Jesus gave the church Apostles to Govern. These anointed men and women give direction and offer leadership to a church, group of churches, or a group of ministers.

He gave us Prophets to Guide. They release anointing and share insights. These individuals have intolerance for unscriptural behavior and are used of the Holy Spirit to give supernatural direction to the Body of Christ.

Evangelists Gather. They have a charisma that draws men and women to a saving knowledge of Jesus. These individuals often flow in supernatural anointing to reveal the power of God to both the skeptical and the uncertain by the working of miracles.

Pastors Guard. The pastor is most often described as a "shepherd." The shepherd of the local church is responsible for the care and feeding of the sheepfold. He protects them from wolves and sees to it they are fed a balanced faith diet.

Teachers Ground. Teachers impart Biblical truth that stirs hunger for more of this truth. They are responsible for working in conjunction with pastors to create and maintain doctrinal equilibrium within the congregation.

Everything you need to succeed is in the church.

Since your success is guaranteed, act like it!

Choose a home church and stay connected.

Wisdom Declaration: "I will wear a smile today because the enemy of my life is a defeated foe. Jesus won victory over him on Mt. Calvary.No chains of bondage are holding me back from success in the Kingdom. Father, thank you for giving the church Apostles, Prophets, Evangelists, Pastors and Teachers to help me grow in the things of God. I choose to walk in freedom."

23

Forgive To Release Financial Favor

Financial Favor Is Vital.

I grew up around financially ignorant folk.

Most in my area worked at hard manual labor jobs.

During personal testimony time they would routinely state how they considered money to be unimportant.

Let me truthfully tell you the exact opposite. Money is more important than anyone else is telling you.

Some years ago I was attempting to connect through the Dallas-Fort Worth Airport back to my Houston, Texas home area. Thunderstorms are a big problem for us in the spring and summer months and this night was no different. A storm cell so high and wide it could not be flown over or around was blocking our flight path

I was booked on the last flight out. I was determined to be on that plane and back with my congregation in the morning.

As the evening dragged on, I became hungry. Let me confess: I love hotdogs. I have heard all the health arguments and do not disagree. I know...*but I still love hotdogs!*

As I ordered I talked with the young woman behind the

counter, I became interested in her life story and began to ask a few questions. She was a committed Christian who served in the youth ministry of her denominational church.

She was also the divorced mom of three young boys who was working the extra job because her ex-husband had disappeared. No child support was flowing into her life.

Gently, I asked if she was a tither and she assured me she was. So, I told her the Bible teaches the tithe will open open the windows of heaven and position us for an overflow blessing. I offered to pray.

Quickly, she announced, "No need to pray for me. We're getting by OK. Besides, money is not really important. Everything would be fine if that jerk of an ex-husband would just pay child support."

Bingo! The light of pain began to shine. As we spoke more, I found someone so wounded as to be completely unwilling to forgive. Eventually, I flew home with the knowledge that the river of God's blessing had no real chance of flowing in her life because of unforgiveness and hostility.

In the Full-Gospel movement we quickly quote Luke 6:38, *"Give and it shall be given unto you, good measure, pressed down, and shaken together, and running over shall men give into your bosom. For with the same measure you mete it shall be given back to you."*

Tragically few know the qualifier is found in Luke 6:37, *"Judge not, and you shall not be judged. Condemn not, and you shall not be condemned. Forgive, and you will be forgiven."*

Your prosperity may not be flowing.

If so, unforgiveness may be hampering your financial increase.

Assess your life for a moment. Is there someone you need to forgive?

Wisdom Declaration: "Father, I forgive so I can be forgiven. Your plan is that I live in financial abundance so I can take care of my family, create a legacy for my grandchildren, and fund the work of God around the earth. Reveal hidden heart attitudes that may be blocking the blessings of God from flowing in my life. I ask for these things and call them done in the Name of Jesus. Amen. It is done!"

24

Constantly Feed Your Faith

Evangelist R.W. Schambach Is In Heaven Today.

He was an old-school Pentecostal preacher who flamboyantly preached and lived a life and message of miracles.

"Brother Schambach" will be forever remembered for saying, "You don't have any problems. All you need is faith in God."

Yes, we do have challenges in life. However, as Brother Schambach was saying, compared to the goodness of God, the issues we face are nothing.

"God Seemingly Does Nothing On Earth Apart From Faith," –John Wesley. Let this ancient statement flood your consciousness.

Pastor Roscoe Hilliard is an exceptional preacher and a brilliant illustrator. His depiction of our misplaced frustration with God touched my heart in a deep way.

"We stand around, shuffling our feet, angrily looking upward with an attitude of, "When are you going to do something? Big Mama took care of the entire neighborhood. She made sure everyone was always fed. Now she is sick and you are not doing anything about it."

He then said, "All the while Jesus is looking down saying, 'I'm waiting on somebody to speak some faith!'"

Faith Is The Currency of The Kingdom.

Our faith must be an ever increasing thing. Because of this the Apostle Peter gives us tremendous insight into the necessity of constantly focusing upon building our faith. "But also for this very reason, giving all diligence, add to your faith virtue, to virtue knowledge, to knowledge self-control, to self-control perseverance, to perseverance godliness, to godliness brotherly kindness, and to brotherly kindness love," (2 Peter 1:5-7).

Seven Additions To Faith

1. Virtue – Righteous behavior that demonstrates our faith.

2. Knowledge – Understanding of the things of God.

3. Self-control – Requiring the soul and body to submit to The Word.

4. Perseverance – Continuing in godly living...*even during hard times.*

5. Godliness – Gladly living the Jesus lifestyle.

6. Brotherly kindness – Demonstrating the same high-quality patience and compassion one would display toward a family member.

7. Love – The type of deep, abiding type of affection our Lord has for us.

Reject condemnation.

Receive more deposits of faith.

This isn't about what you haven't done.

This is about something we all need to do more of.

We all need to give God something to work with, by stating what we believe and expect.

Wisdom Declaration: This is the day you have made, Lord. I choose to rejoice and be glad in the fact I can add more faith to my faith. I will grow in knowledge of You today. My strength will increase in every area of my life. The Kingdom will be a better place because I am in it. I choose to move from faith to faith, and from glory to even more glory. My faith is strong and getting stronger today…and everyday!

25

Recognize You Are In A Faith Fight

We Live in a War Zone.

The Bible is clear on this point.

It is unpleasantly clear to my point of view.

Honestly, the fact we are not really fighting people makes this war even more treacherous.

I don't get angry easily, but when I do, I have a tendency to want to hang on to the offense. It is not my first instinct to believe the fight is not really with another human being. Even so, the Bible explains, *"For we do not wrestle against flesh and blood, but against principalities, against powers, against the rulers of the darkness of this age, against spiritual hosts of wickedness in the heavenly places,"* (Ephesians 6:12).

Yes, the attack usually comes through a person. However, our fight is never really with a human being. Not even when that human is demonically inspired to misbehave.

People may misbehave, but our issue is not with them. It is with the demon spirit motivating them.

Difference Comes With A Price.

The forgiving person is truly unique. Years ago I was in love with a woman who was (likely is) the most forgiving person I have ever met.

I thought it was a personality trait. Over time I learned it was a choice.

The caterpillar fights to become something better. My friend's nature was really one of combat, but she wanted to be a butterfly.

Her first response to offense was to lash out. It was only through years of renewing her mind through the washing of the water of the Word of God (read Ephesians 5:6) that she became victorious over what she called "temper fits."

Your move toward something more in life will require the fight of faith.

The fight of faith brings with it a level of discomfort.

The result of the fight is worth the effort.

Are you ready to be a champion?

Wisdom Declaration: "I do not expect offense to come my way today, but if it does I will be ready. I will not lash out. I will be patient. I will behave in a way that honors Jesus. I refuse to see my struggle as being with a person, but as part of the warfare between the kingdoms of light and darkness. The fight of faith is one of graciousness. I will be gracious because the Word of God lives big in me."

26

Refuse Confusion

We Can Trust Jesus.

He is the epitome of truth and stability.

Satan exists for the sole purpose of confusing people.

The Bible says satan is a liar and truth cannot be found anywhere in him.

He injects confusion into the unsaved to make them think life is hopeless. During their dark nights of the soul he tells these hurting individuals there is no God. He piles doubt on top of doubt.

For those who believe there is a God, satan works to convince them of their unworthiness. He tells them their lifestyle of bad choices disqualifies them from ever knowing God.

His attacks do not stop when we become believers. The attack just takes on a different form. The attack comes from another direction.

He can no longer hit us about our condition. Our condition is no longer that of "sinner". Our identification has completely changed.

We are part of the royal family. Our position has changed.

Consider this astonishingly powerful statement of who we are in Him, *"To Him who loved us and washed us from our sins in His own blood, ⁶and has made us kings and priests to His God and Father, to Him be glory and dominion forever and ever. Amen,"* (Revelation 5B-6).

This is not something that will happen in the future. This is right now! We are kings and priests in the Kingdom of God. We are part of the Royal Family of God.

When we goof up in some way that displeases the Lord, satan comes again with the attack that focuses on our old condition. He is not stupid. He knows or our position. He also knows our weaknesses.

These attacks are all focus breakers.

Anyone Or Anything That Breaks Your Focus Has The Potential Of Becoming An Enemy of God's Plan For Your Life.

Focus breakers are to be avoided at all cost. These individuals and situations exist to inject confusion into your life. If confusion cannot stop you, it stills slow you down.

Evaluate Your Relationships.

As a pastor, this was a hard skill master. Yet, I had to learn how. The revelation came when a particular person left my presence and I noticed confusion was working me over.

In that moment I realized that individual was comfortable with confusion. As unkind as it may sound, for the sake of my family and congregation I limited that individuals time with me.

Your condition has changed.

Your new position in Christ overrules all the past.

Wisdom Declaration: "I am a new creation in Christ. My old condition has passed away. My position is among the redeemed. I have been bought back from sin and satan by the precious blood of Jesus. I will not receive confusion about who I am or where I am going. My purpose is certain because my relationship with God is secure. I will work with a clear mind free of confusion. I will understand all my relationships for what they are. I will think the thoughts of God today because His Word is living in me."

27

Do Not Make Life Harder Than It Has To Be

Jesus Defined Our Role.

He defined His own role, too.

The Apostle John recorded how Jesus described both, *"I am the vine, you are the branches,"* (John 16:8a)

Jesus didn't tell us, "I am the vine. You go out there and try to be the branches." No, this is our position. We are already the branches. There is no struggle in being a branch.

Because we have received Jesus we are in Jesus. We do not have to try to find acceptance in the church. The grace He imparted to us at the time of our salvation immediately made us *"...accepted in The Beloved,"* (Ephesians 1:6b)

All we are required to do is live as a reflection of our position in Him. When we do position ourselves in such a way that our lives declare our position in Christ our productivity and success in His Kingdom are guaranteed. Jesus made the promise, *"He who abides in Me and I in him, bears much fruit..."* (John 16:8b).

We can do all things through faith in our Lord and the promises in His Word. Yet, Jesus makes a telling point about our need for His ongoing ministry by the power of by The Holy Spirit, *"Without Me you can do nothing,"* (John 16:8c).

When God sees us He is looking through the lens of the blood of Jesus. He sees us in the new position we accepted through believing in Jesus as Savior and Lord.

On the day I was born again, no one had to tell me what had happened. I knew. English theologian Martin Loyd-Jones calls this, "The instant and direct witness of The Holy Spirit that confirms we belong to Christ."

Dr. Loyd-Jones bases his belief on personal experience and the writings of the Beloved Physician, Luke. Dr. Luke wrote, *"The Spirit Himself bears witness with our spirit that we are children of God, and if children, then heirs—heirs of God and joint heirs with Christ, if indeed we suffer with Him, that we may also be glorified together,"* (Romans 8:16-17).

Quoting Dauphin Charles, "I am royalty and I shan't behave any other way."

When Father God looks at us, He sees a family member,

Don't make life harder than it has to be.

Take your place in the family.

Assert yourself.

> **Wisdom Declaration:** "I am thankful for the revelation of who I am in The Kingdom of God. I will walk as royalty today. I will hold my head high, my gaze will be clear. Everything I view is territory to be conquered and occupied for The Kingdom. I will boldly walk in authority. I am both a king and a priest on the earth. I will use my spiritual authority to live in liberty and free those held captive. My future is a bright one because I know who I am."

28

Honor The Law of The Seed

Seed Is Anything I Have.

Anything I have can become more.

Something I have can create what I desire.

My life is a warehouse of Seed. My smile is the Seed for favor. The gentle words I sow create a climate of peace.

God notices my every righteous act. The financial Seed I sow into the work of God today creates the future I desire.

I choose to "buck the trend" and declare I believe God desires that I prosper in every area of my life. He is especially concerned that I prosper financially so I can help further the reach of His Kingdom.

King Solomon, the richest man who ever lived, had remarkable insight into financial matters. He encouraged sowing financial Seed to create a supernatural covering of protection. By doing so you protect yourself against "evil days". *"Cast your bread upon the waters, For you will find it after many days. Give a serving to seven, and also to eight, For you do not know what evil will be on the earth,"* (Ecclesiastes 11:1).

Do not allow what you see to stop you from sowing. We all go through times when it seems our service to God is producing little. In those times, double down!

Note Solomon's warning to those who consider circumstances rather than the certain promises of God, *"He who observes the wind will not sow, and he who regards the clouds will not reap,"* (Ecclesiastes 11:4).

Keep your focus on The Word and Spirit of God. We cannot allow times of darkness to keep us from sowing.

I pray that you will recognize the difference your harvest. Solomon warns us that paying too much attention to circumstances will also keep us from reaping what God has given.

As appreciative as I am of King Solomon's insights, we have a better understanding of sowing and reaping than He did. He was advocating sowing in many directions because he felt we couldn't really know what would work. *"In the morning sow your seed, And in the evening do not withhold your hand; For you do not know which will prosper, Either this or that, Or whether both alike will be good,"* (Ecclesiastes 11:6).

Thank God we live under a better covenant. It contains better promises. *"But now He has obtained a more excellent ministry, inasmuch as He is also Mediator of a better covenant, which was established on better promises,"* (Hebrews 8:6).

Everything I do in faith will produce a harvest of faith.

I do not just act in faith, I have the spirit of faith. *"And since we have the same spirit of faith, according to what is written, "I believed and therefore I spoke," we also believe and therefore speak,"* (2 Corinthians 4:13).

As I speak what I believe, the creative ability of God is released. The financial Seed I have sown into the work of

The Kingdom becomes more when I water it with words of faith.

Wisdom Declaration: "The greater one lives in me. I have the spirit of faith. I know God wants me to prosper. He enjoys the prosperity of His servants. I am a tither and a giver. The Seed has left the barn known as my bank account. It is in the field of God's Kingdom. It is creating more of what it is. As the Bible says, I declare that I will live in prosperity and pleasure all the days of my life. The lives of untold numbers of people will be changed forever because of my generosity. The generous soul will prosper. The spirit of generosity is living in me. The spirit of generosity will motivate me today and every day."

29

Consider Your Location

Places Matter To God.

Location Is Very Important.

God created places before He created people.

There is a place where you will prosper. There is a place where you will decline.

When considering real estate we remember the three most important things are location, location and location. The congregation I served as pastor was given a piece of land where we built our sanctuary and educational facilities. It was never an ideal location for a church, but God prospered us there..

After using the property as long as we could, we sold it and relocated to a more conducive area. The Hilton Corporation found our old spot to be an ideal location for one of their hotel brands.

Abraham would still be idol-worshipping Abram had he not heeded God's instruction to leave where he was living. God commanded, *"Get out of your country, from your family and from your father's house, To a land that I will show you,"* (Genesis 12:1).

God's desire for us is always greater than we see. God desired that Abram become "more" than he was, but it required leaving the place of security and comfort.

"I will make you a great nation; I will bless you and make your name great," (Genesis 12:2a).

We are blessed to be a blessing. God desires to increase us so we can minister increase to others. *"And you shall be a blessing. ³I will bless those who bless you, and I will curse him who curses you; And in you all the families of the earth shall be blessed,"* (Genesis 12:2b-3).

The staggering promise of God to Abraham is ours today. *"And if you are Christ's, then you are Abraham's seed, and heirs according to the promise,"* (Galatians 3:29).

Yet, none of this would have come to pass without Abram's willingness to leave where he was for the place of increase. In the new location God even changed his name to from Abram (high father) to Abraham (father of multitudes).

God always has something better for His people. Many fail to achieve because they are unwilling to make geographical change. I will not pretend this is easy.

One of the biggest challenges of my lifetime involved leaving Houston for ministry in New Orleans. Yet, that time in New Orleans was one of powerful change for me. I learned to hear and obey the voice of God in an entirely new dimension.

This promise of blessing for being in the right location is for all Christians, *"For you are all sons of God through faith in Christ Jesus. ²⁷For as many of you as were baptized into Christ have put on Christ. ²⁸There is neither Jew nor Greek, there is neither slave nor free, there is neither male nor female; for you are all one in Christ Jesus,"* (Galatians 3:26-28).

You may not have to leave where you live.

God may be directing you to a different career path.

He may simply be indicating your need to take in more territory where you already live and work.

Wisdom Declaration: "I agree with today's teaching that location is ultra important in the Kingdom of God. Help me find and function in my "right place". Help me obey the example of willingness set by Abraham. If you require a geographical relocation, I will follow your direction. If you only want me to reposition myself spiritually, I will relocate in that realm. Where you lead me, I will follow. I will go with you all the way. Amen."

30

Learn The Power of Ongoing Forgiveness

Ongoing Relationships Require Ongoing Forgiveness.

Dr. Oral Roberts told me, "Deal with your church the way it really is, rather than how you wish it was." It is the same way with our life.

Life contains realities I do not like. I have no desire to deal with them, but they are there demanding attention.

Apologies will be necessary. I am reminded of a quote I have used often. It came to me without attribution, which I regret as I would like to honor such a thoughtful person by recognizing their deposit of truth into my life.

"The first to apologize is bravest. The first to forgive is the strongest. The first to forget is the happiest." –Unknown.

As believers we are to be like our Lord. He not only forgives, He chooses to forget. *"Then he adds: "Their sins and lawless acts I will remember no more,"* (Hebrews 10:17).

Proverbs is one of the two wisdom books of the Bible, James being the other. In Proverbs 10:12 we read, *"Hatred stirs up strife, But love covers all sins."* Love does not just forgive, love endeavors to forget.

My maternal grandfather was jailed for vagrancy. This

event took place during the Great Depression. He was in St. Louis looking for work when he was arrested for "having no visible means of support."

There was no sin involved in this event. So far as I can see there was not even any element of wrongdoing. Yet, one of my cousins held this against our grandfather. Each time my grandfather spoke to us my cousin would say softly, "How can you believe a jailbird?"

He was offended by our grandfather's past and refused to let it go. He harbored bitterness toward him throughout my grandfather's lifetime.

One of my church members, a C.P.A., has been a member of my spiritual father's congregation. She had been arrested, tried and convicted of fraud before becoming part of my congregation.

During conversation one day she said, "I need to get home. I promised God if he would get me out of prison I would stop working long hours and enjoy my family."

I said nothing to her, but mentioned it to Dr. Smith the next time I saw him. What he revealed shocked me. She had stolen money from multiple churches she represented... *and his was one of them.*

"Why didn't you tell me?" I asked.

"I have forgiven her," was his open reply.

Then he said something remarkable, "I forgave her each time I saw her until I stopped thinking of it."

Ongoing Relationships Will Require Ongoing Forgiveness.

Wisdom Declaration: "In advance of offense, I choose to live a life of forgiveness. My relationships will not be destroyed by offense. I will not hold others in a place of sin and failure simply because I do not wish to be held there myself. Just like Jesus, I will be known as a forgiving individual."

31

Respect The Law of Honor

Honor Is The Key of Access.

Honor can get you into any atmosphere.

Dishonor can keep you from those who would promote you.

Satan was once called Lucifer. His original name means "Collector of Honor." Lucifer collected the worship (honor) of the inhabitants in the heavenly realm and presented it back to the Father.

Once I learned this truth, I saw the problem present in so many worship teams. Instead of offering the glory back to the Father, too many receive the gifts of honor as their own. They see the acts of worship as something they have produced rather than being something God desires and deserves.Such and attitude is clearly something that dishonors God, and the call upon the life of the individual.

I plan to live a long time? Why? I have honored my parents. *"Honor your father and your mother, that your days may be long upon the land which the Lord your God is giving you,"* (Exodus 20:12).

In Luke 14 Jesus gives a pointed example of the price of failing to properly honor others. *"When you are invited by anyone to a wedding feast, do not sit down in the best place, lest one more honorable than you be invited by him; ⁹and he who invited you and him come and say to you, 'Give place to this man,' and then you begin with shame to take the lowest place. ¹⁰But when you are invited, go and sit down in the lowest place, so that when he who invited you comes he may say to you, 'Friend, go up higher.' Then you will have glory in the presence of those who sit at the table with you. ¹¹For whoever exalts himself will be humbled, and he who humbles himself will be exalted,"* (Luke 14:7-11).

I exalted myself once.

The result was unforgettably painful.

I was a reporter for The Houston Chronicle. I had the delight of helping one of the beat writers cover the Houston Astros. He was an older man who had trouble walking. In those pre-cellular phone days, due to his infirmity, I would take a list of his questions down to the clubhouse to ask players and coaches questions about the events of the game.

The first person I spoke with in a major league clubhouse was Baseball Hall of Fame© outfielder Willie Mays. I was much more awed than he.

When baseball season was over I returned to college full-time and worked part-time for the newspaper. One of the "perks" was free admission to different events.

The Houston Oilers were scheduled to play "Broadway Joe" Namath and The New York Jets at The Astrodome. My seat was OK, but not a premier one. I was in the section where customized sandwiches were served, but I noticed two empty seats in the front row reserved for Cal Thomas.

Cal was a reporter for the NBC affiliate in Houston. We

were acquainted. The night before I had seen him on the network covering the Republican Convention in Miami where President Richard Nixon was nominated for re-election.

It only made sense to move up to the seats reserved for Cal and his wife. Little did I know but Continental, American, Eastern and Braniff Airlines all flew hourly flights from Miami to Houston.

You can guess the rest. Cal and his wife walked in to find me eating steak at their front row seats. They laughed. Security didn't.

Respecting protocol is one of the proofs of honor.

God honors those who demonstrate honor.

The rules of the house matter.

Wisdom Declaration: "I will live my life as a person of honor. Above all things I will honor my God by honoring His Word. His Word forms the ultimate protocol for my life. I will honor my employer, my family, friends and co-workers. The honor I sow into others will cause me to be honored."

CPSIA information can be obtained
at www.ICGtesting.com
Printed in the USA
FFHW012059090519
52369381-57768FF